Juan Carlos Jimenez

Supreme Art
50 Best Practices in Customer Care

Published by Cograf
Caracas, Venezuela - December 2010

Supreme Art
50 Best Practices in Customer Care
Original book published in spanish, title "Arte Supremo. 50 prácticas de buena atención al cliente"

Author: Juan Carlos Jimenez
Facebook: jucarjim - cograf
Twitter: @jucarjim - @cograf

ISBN: 1482799332

Published by Cograf
www.libroscograf.com
Facebook: www.facebook.com/cograf
Twitter: @cograf

Av. Francisco de Miranda con Av. Principal de Los Ruices, Centro Empresarial Miranda, Piso 1, Ofic 1K. Los Ruices. Caracas 1070, Venezuela. Telf/Fax: (+58 +212) 237-9702
Rif: J-30336261-3 - E-mail: contactocograf@cograf.com
www.cograf.com

Supreme art earns applause

Art is exciting. Art is moving. Art is notable. It draws our attention and captivates us.

Artistic achievement dazzles us, it touches our soul, it fascinates us and motivates us to applaud and shout: "Yay!", "Bravo!", "Wow!"

Artists transform what it ordinary into something extraordinary. They make complex tasks appear simple, easy to do and even fun. What's more, they do it with passion and joy. So, it's understandable why artistic work doesn't go unnoticed.

Applauding the artist is a form of tribute, a show of appreciation and a gesture of admiration for this person who has inspired us.

Artists influence our moods, overcoming the indifference, monotony, inattention and habitualness in our lives. Their artistic work is superior to common, everyday, average work.

Artists demand much more from themselves. They aren't satisfied with work that is simply good; they want to do something that is "out of this world", something notable. They make a deliberate effort to move, to excite and to win applause.

From a professional point of view, it is especially interesting and useful to think of your work as an art form, because you could compare it, instead, to other types of work. This perspective will enable you to determine whether or not your work elicits emotion and applause, and whether or not you perform it like an artist.

Providing customer care like an artist is a big challenge, even for the best of us. It is a level of professionalism that can only be reached when we make the personal decision to do so. However, this artistic perspective is even broader and more significant when we begin thinking in terms of "supreme art".

This is an idea inspired by the award-winning Roberto Benigni film, "Life is Beautiful". The main character, Guido, learns a universal lesson from his uncle while he is training him to work at his hotel: "Service is a supreme art. God serves man, but this doesn't mean that He becomes man's servant".

How many times have you read or heard that the work of serving others is so supreme that it resembles God's work? Without a doubt, this is a special way of honoring this type of work, but it is also very appropriate considering the complexities involved in customer care.

There tends to be a lot of resistance and social blackmail standing in the way of personal proactiveness. However, if it is taken up as a supreme art, then it becomes work that is worthy of our efforts.

Providing people with full, exceptional attention does not make us servants, but instead makes us extraordinary professionals and better people.

"Supreme Art" is also a book that gives us the opportunity to reflect and learn about customer care with an air of elegance and distinction.

In these pages, I encourage you each day to renew the dignity that exists in every act of good service, from the smallest to the most significant.

If you would like to discuss your impressions of the ideas presented in this book, please write to me at jucar@cograf.com. It would be my pleasure to address any comments you may have.

Juan Carlos Jimenez
December, 2010

Contents

Service isn't the same thing as care

In this book, you will find 50 examples of specific behaviors that characterize **good customer care**. One of my objectives is for you to understand the difference between providing a service and providing excellent care. That way you will be able to improve your performance immediately.

Most people who work in the world of service are not aware of these differences. If they were, they would provide better care. Simply because of this lack of awareness, many customers routinely receive poor attention from numerous companies and organizations.

For example, it is hard for customers to feel like they are receiving good care when an employee is writing text messages or using the computer without ever looking up to establish eye contact.

Simply doing one's job isn't enough. Providing care has to do with the quantity and quality of **true attention** that you pay to **your** customers. Most people who arrive at an understanding of what is involved in actual customer care derive great personal satisfaction from their work. Feeling useful through helping people gives them a sense of wellbeing in every aspect.

Why do I say "true attention?" It's because customers are very aware of the difference between attention that is forced and attention that is **obviously** given without annoyance or bitterness.

In terms of customer care, the concept of "true" is similar to the concept of "total quality". True attention is authentic, reliable, credible, genuine, demonstrable and timely; it leaves no doubts and it is offered **with pleasure**.

This is why eye contact, to give just one example, is so important to customers. If a customer is standing in front of you and you don't make eye contact, he or she **will feel** that your attention and acknowledgement are only partial. So, it would be very difficult for him or her to feel like you are providing great customer care.

Another purpose of this book is for you to identify and understand the difference between "taking care" of customers and simply "serving" them.

Most people tend to use these words interchangeably, and that is find. But, well-prepared **professionals** know when and why to make a distinction between the two.

"Service" is what is provided by you and the company you work for

For example, at a bank, they not only **provide** financial products, but information as well, and customers can be served through various channels: branches, call centers, ATM machines, email and websites. All of this is part of the bank's services.

In the case of a restaurant, service consists of the quality of the food they **serve**, but also the amount of time they take to serve it, the menu variety, the prices, the demeanor of the servers and other staff and the cleanliness of the restrooms.

In a telephone company or cable TV company, service signifies the quality of the connection, but also the amount of time they take to address customer requests and concerns and what the employees say (or don't say) when addressing them.

In any type of company, service also signifies timeliness, the **fulfillment** of everything that is promised and the image that is presented, whether through the company's facilities and resources or the appearance of its products and employees. This is why it is somewhat inappropriate to have a "Customer Service Department", because everything a company does or doesn't do eventually translates into customer service.

That is, service isn't simply the exclusive aspect of one department in the company. And this is the reason why you often have to help people resolve complaints arising in different departments of the company you work for.

However, there are some aspects of service that depend on **your individual** decision and initiative:

1. Your personal appearance and hygiene.

2. Your professional training and awareness of how you communicate (both verbally and non-verbally).

3. Your level of knowledge about the company in which you work and all of its operations and products.

4. The quality of the information you give customers at **all** times.

Here begins the difference between "service" and "customer care".

"Care" is the way you serve

The quality of care is determined by your personal decision as to **how you work**: how you behave, how you proceed, how you listen, how you look at people, how you speak, how you sit and how you walk, regardless of the specific type of service you provide.

The resources companies have in place for providing service only come alive through you and your way of working.

That is, good customer care depends 100% on **how you have decided** to do your work and fulfill your professional responsibilities.

The company establishes the infrastructure that makes service possible, but you are the one who provides it. In other words, **you are the care**.

This principle explains why customers who are dissatisfied with the service they received earlier can be very satisfied with the care you give them. For example:

* If someone asks you for information and you answer that you don't know, you can promise to find out and let the customer know within a specified timeframe. That depends on your decision.

* If the resolution of a problem doesn't depend on you or your department, you can still **take care** of the customer and **help** him or her by becoming a representative of the corresponding person or department. That also depends on your decision.

I'm not saying that care is more important than service. I'm only trying to demonstrate why it is so important for you to understand *the difference you make*.

Ensuring good service is the responsibility of every company and part of your professional duties. But, excellent customer care is something personal that you decide on, and this is the main focus of this book.

In this spirit, each one of the 50 good customer care practices you will find in this book is intended to provide you with guidance in order to strengthen and dignify your day-to-day work.

Why 50 practices?

I suggest that you use this book as an annual **training** plan. Although there are 50 practices, I recommend that evaluate yourself every six months. That way you can spread it out evenly over the 52 weeks of the year.

1) During the first week, quickly skim over the 50 practices and evaluate how often you employ each one:
1 = Never
2 = Almost never
3 = Sometimes
4 = Almost always
5 = It's a habit

This exercise will serve as a point of departure, showing you the **opportunities** for adjustments and improvements in the quality of care you provide.

If you would like to get even more out of it, ask your boss or a coworker to evaluate you. In general, they will be more objective than you.

Furthermore, your boss' responses will give you immediate guidance for reconciling your performance with what he or she expects of you.

2) On the basis of this evaluation, start developing one practice each week.

In this case, "develop" means read the practice, reread it, think about it and share **your thoughts** on its meanings and implications. If it is an idea you're already familiar with, take advantage of the opportunity to renew it, **review it** and expand on it.

3) On Week 26 (after six months), reevaluate yourself first 25 practices. This way you will be aware of your progress, as well as the areas that still need improvement.

4) On Week 27, continue developing one practice per week, starting with #26, until you reach Week 52.

5) The following year, repeat the whole cycle.

Remember that the habit of maintaining, renewing and practicing these behaviors on a consistent basis is like **a gym** for your commitment to good customer service.

To get better results from this book

In this book, you will find some new ideas and others that you are probably already aware of. The goal here isn't simply to acquire knowledge, but instead to translate your knowledge, both new and existing, into the renewal of old, good habits and the implementation of new habits in the performance of your work.

You know that any knowledge that isn't periodically refreshed is forgotten and that repetitive activities, if they become unconscious routines, turn you into a "robot".

In customer care, it is indispensable to be aware of this because taking good care of people requires a significant investment of energy, which makes it emotionally draining.

Renewing your good customer care practices on a daily basis is the most efficient way to boost your spirits and keep them in top form.

1. Share your thoughts

After reading and rereading each practice, talk to others about the aspects you find most interesting. It's a simple but very effective exercise because it forces you to dig deeper and expand on those ideas in your own words.

Sharing your thoughts with others implies structuring the ideas in your mind in such a way that you can communicate them intelligibly.

The process of **reflecting and verbalizing** your thoughts empowers your intellectual ability to analyze and synthesize. It won't take much time, just 10 or 15 minutes each day.

Choose two or three ideas that interest you from each practice and share them with your coworkers, friends or family, whether because the ideas seem novel or different to you or simply because they arouse your curiosity.

2. Reread the content of each practice

You have a whole week to develop a practice. During this time, you should read it at least once a day. It's a basic review exercise that has the power to stimulate your creativity.

Read to increase your understanding and do it at a time when you're calm and can enjoy the act of reading and renewing the ideas that you are studying and assimilating.

Reading should be a habit. Don't be anxious due to time constraints. What you can read in 10 minutes is enough, as long as you do it every day. As time goes by, you will realize that this short period of time is very productive if it is consistent.

It might be more comfortable for you to read before you go to sleep. However, if you usually feel very tired by the end of the day, read in the mornings when your mind is rested, fresh and uncluttered.

To make your reading and studying easier, the practices I provide in this book only take up two pages each, so you can read them without tiring.

3. Put your thoughts in writing

When you read about a practice, take notes on the thoughts it inspires and the situations in which you can use it to improve your customer care.

If you think about them and verbalize your thoughts, this becomes a very effective intellectual exercise for increasing your analytic and creative abilities, and **writing down the ideas the reading inspires** is even more powerful.

Don't let time constraints or the quality and quantity of what you write become sources of anxiety. Work at your own pace, but make sure to do it every day.

Dedicating a few moments of your ten-minute reading session to making quick notes on what you're reading can produce big results.

The point isn't for you to write a summary, an essay or an article, although it is likely that, in time, you will end up writing something similar if you practice every day. The important thing is to take notes on what you read so that you can "think in writing".

It might be an interesting idea to write your thoughts in an email to share them with another person. If that makes writing easier for you, do it.

Allow me to rephrase a reflection of the Indian leader, Mahatma Gandhi (http://bit.ly/V8e20U), which provides a broad perspective on the importance of "practice" and review in learning processes:

"Mind your thoughts because they become your words. Mind your words because they become your actions. Mind your actions because they become your habits. Mind your habits because they become your values. Mind your values because they become your destiny".

1 | Work for people

Everything that is done in any organization, whether private or public, is geared toward satisfying people's needs.

Depending on your workplace, you can observe this more or less clearly. If you work in an area or department that is far away from the "front desk", it's likely that sometimes you say, "I don't deal with customers".

In any case, there's no mistake about it: **everything you do** in your job affects the lives of the company's customers, either directly or indirectly, without exceptions.

In this sense, whatever your specific job duties may be, the core of your work revolves around your customers.

Your professional duties and responsibilities are simply a means of satisfying them.

The customer may be a company or an institution, but in the end, it is a person or group of people that uses whatever is produced by the company you work for or that is provided by you directly.

A lot of poor service arises from forgetting this principle because people end up focusing more on the manual aspects of their specific duties than on the people who are affected by their work.

If you neglect to greet customers, fail to use their names or talk to them without looking at them while you read something on your cell phone or computer, this is often the result of forgetting that you work for people.

People who work in company departments where they don't have direct contact with the public often state that they "don't deal with customers". They forget that their coworkers are "internal customers", who also depend on their quality attention and service.

Your work is not defined by your job title or the college degree you have earned. The essence of your work is the people that benefit directly or indirectly from what you do. In four words: you work for people.

2 | Serve with dignity

Dignity is synonymous with excellence, integrity, nobility and honor.

Dignity means behaving like a person.

Working with dignity is the main source of professional fulfillment and personal wellbeing.

It's true that you can't always choose the work you would most like to do. However, you can always choose to work with enthusiasm and dignity.

If you decide that your work isn't sufficiently dignified, your daily performance will be characterized by annoyance, apathy, monotony and bitterness.

If you fail to understand that the dignity of your behavior is the essential ingredient for providing people with good service, at times you will lose the focus of your work and won't concentrate on the people you are helping.

Dignity enables you to understand that angry customers manage to offend or disrespect only those who choose to feel offended or disrespected or those who fail to understand that they work for people. As a consequence, in their concept of their work, helping customers isn't the first priority.

If you work with an awareness of the **dignity of helping people**, it's easier for you to understand that most customers are angered by the poor service and care they received before they came to you.

This is precisely why you are the one that has the opportunity to provide them with good attention and positively influence their mood.

Providing good service is the most dignified work of all because, more than any other, it requires you to value yourself, what you do and other people.

You will only serve people fully when you decide to believe that doing so is important to you and worthy of your efforts. If you feel that **giving people good service dignifies you** as a human being and makes you useful, you will derive pleasure from doing it.

Remember what I told you at the beginning of this book: serving people is so noble, dignified and supreme that it resembles God's work. In the film, "Life is Beautiful", Guido's uncle put it this way: "God serves man, but this doesn't mean that He becomes man's servant".

3 | Your job is to help

The essence of good customer care is **helping people, and helping them means cooperating** with them so they can satisfy their needs.

You contribute to satisfying customers' needs in many ways, depending on your specific job duties.

Whatever your position may be, the quality of the help you provide is determined by the quality of the attention you give.

You are helpful and you provide good care to the extent that **you support** the process of addressing customers' requests or needs, regardless of your specific professional role in that process.

In this sense, you don't only help when you can offer exactly what is asked of you. In fact, your collaboration can be even more significant when you are asked to do something that is obviously "out of your reach".

In those cases **you become part of the solution** whenever you make an enthusiastic effort to give the customer guidance as to how, where and through whom his or her needs can be satisfied.

Helping is **contributing** to solutions, **aiding**, **assisting**, **lending a hand**, **facilitating**, **offering input** and **participating** in the responses customers are seeking, regardless of whether or not this is directly related to your job duties.

Remember that you work for people and this work consists of helping them.

However, in order to help customers, it is indispensable to provide them with good service. This means that:

• You give them your full attention, listening without annoyance or bitterness.

• You really understand what they need.

• You enjoy helping people.

• You want to do it.

All of this depends on your personal decision.

Helping people with a great sense of dignity makes you a better person and a better professional. However, it's your decision.

4 | You can always help

Don't believe even for a second that you can and should only help customers if what they are asking for is part of your job duties or those of your department.

When this happens, you end up giving poor attention and making **excuses** for not helping:

–This department doesn't handle that...

–I'm not the person who deals with that...

–The person in charge of that isn't here right now...

–We don't have that product at the moment...

–The person who can help you isn't here yet...

These types of excuses and "justifications" lead customers to believe that you simply don't feel like helping them, don't want to deal with them or that you have other priorities.

If they make a request that isn't part of your specific job duties or department, your professional responsibility at that moment is the following:

1) **Face** the customer and really listen to what he or she is saying.

2) **Verify** that you understand his or her needs correctly.

3) **Provide** useful information to facilitate satisfying those needs.

Helping often means going with the customer. If the request is new, unfamiliar or too complex for you, simply relaying information isn't enough.

To provide a real good experience, sometimes you have to go with the customer to the appropriate department or person (which gives you an excellent opportunity to learn more about your work).

Other times you have to call another department to alert them of the situation so that the customer doesn't have to repeat the whole story to the next person he or she talks to.

As you can see, ***providing good service is helping***, and this is done by focusing on what you can do and what is within your reach.

5 | No one can force you to give good customer care

No one can obligate you to appreciate people or help them. Nothing in the world can force you to like or enjoy the job of giving people good customer care.

Job duties, personal concern or financial difficulties can sometimes lead you to be **obedient and fake** when you provide service to your customers, as if you were simply reading a script.

This is why we have people who greet us saying, "Good afternoon", while their faces are saying that they are upset or that there is nothing good at all about the afternoon.

They fulfill their obligation of greeting us and perform their work the same way: out of obligation and **without vitality**.

How you feel about what you do and who you are affects your customers more than anything else when you are serving them.

When you provide excellent service, customers feel like **you had the courage** to make the personal decision to do your best to help them. For this reason, **they appreciate you more**, they respect you more, they take an interest in your work and they are more grateful to you.

However, if you only provide service out of obligation, all of your work becomes more difficult and burdensome. Everything that you have to do becomes more complicated and annoying.

Under these circumstances, it is very unlikely that you will really help people or that your customers will feel like you have given them good customer care.

Those people who serve others fully end up deriving enjoyment and satisfaction from what they do. However, their dedication is their personal decision.

It is your decision to give your best when assisting people. You are the master of your will and it is up to you to understand that providing good care is the best opportunity for you to demonstrate your professionalism.

6 | Care with a sense of opportunity

If you learn how to provide customers with good service, *you will always have* more and better opportunities for professional growth.

If you develop the habit of providing good customer care, you end up being more valued as a person, both by your customers and your coworkers, friends and family. Your opportunities for personal growth depend on how you treat people.

This is a logical result. When you provide good service and feel dignified by doing so, you manage to *positively influence* people and you make them feel good because they feel genuinely valued and respected by you.

Good attention is always an opportunity for you to show your *appreciation* of that customer, who chose you and your business over many other options.

The customer could have gone to the competition, but you appreciate the fact that he or she now prefers you and your company and you *acknowledge* that it is thanks to customers like him or her that you have a job. Their presence represents an opportunity for you.

Showing customers that you appreciate them when they are in front of you is the most effective way of making them feel like they matter to you (something which everyone loves to feel).

You show appreciation and respect:

* When you make customers feel welcome in your workplace.

* When you go to them instead of waiting for them to come to you.

* When you ask them how you can help them and you show that you enjoy assisting them.

* When you thank them for their time, for stopping by, for their attention or for their purchase.

These are the ***opportunities*** you have to behave like a true service professional ***every day*** with every customer.

7 | Care with professionalism

A professional is a person who works with the greatest **sense of excellence and quality** on a consistent basis. His or her good performance is constant.

This means that, if you are a professional at what you do, you work with excellence most of the time and not just sometimes.

Professionalism isn't defined by the level of studies you have completed. You can have college degrees and a lot of knowledge, but if you don't put it into practice as you should, most of the time you won't be acknowledged as a professional.

Your professionalism is expressed through your **attitude at work** and the tangible results of what you do. In this sense, confronting the biggest challenges of your work ends up being the "acid test" of your professionalism.

You are a professional because you have made a **commitment to yourself** to give your best in your work, demonstrating that you are honest, responsible and well-prepared for your duties.

The most distinguishing feature of an excellent professional is that he or she **is always** training and learning.

Continuous training is the key to providing superior levels of professionalism, especially in the area of customer care, where it is easy to resign yourself to unconscious work routines that rob your performance of its vitality.

Training with professionalism means refreshing your knowledge so that you **won't underestimate** the basic aspects of your work or take anything for granted.

So, a service professional systematically reviews what he or she already knows and has mastered in order to reconnect with the essentials.

Professionalism in customer care is the result of the dignity you feel when you serve people. This means that you **don't settle** for simply providing a service, but instead, you want your efforts to translate into positive results for the people you help.

8 | Care with artistry

The standards of quality in any artistic discipline are more demanding than those in non-artistic activities. This is why working with artistry **means surpassing average quality**, exceeding expectations and eliciting interest in what you do.

When you don't have an artistic vision of customer care, you end up settling for work that is just "good" or maybe even "so-so" and you place more emphasis on your duties than on the people you're helping.

Outside of art, most people settle for simply fulfilling their obligations and responsibilities. However, good artists, the ones that are memorable, decide to go much further.

A customer care artist is **committed to his or her own personal excellence**, seeking a level of quality in his or her work that manages to move and excite the public, the customers. Make the effort to distinguish your work for being special and out of the ordinary.

When you attend people with artistry, you not only provide them with good service, but also make them feel appreciated, welcome and respected in a special way. This never goes unnoticed by people and almost always garners applause.

Through your actions, your customers will notice, without a doubt, that you enjoy helping them and that you have decided to give your best in order to do so: *you enjoy taking good care of them*.

Customers know that, if you enjoy your work, they will receive more and better assistance from you.

When you work with artistry, you work with more dignity because you are more aware that what you do affects other people's lives.

However, the final analysis of the artistry of your work isn't in your hands, but instead in the hands of your customers. They have the last word. The point isn't for you to believe that you are helping them, but for them to feel that you are.

9 | Distinguish your artistic work

An artist's ability to **fascinate** the public is a direct result of the quantity and quality of his or her artistic training.

You are a customer care artist when you realize that knowledge isn't enough. You can know a lot about your work, but if you don't refresh your knowledge periodically, you run the risk of forgetting it. So, training is equivalent to "refreshing".

This is why **artists do studies**. They do a lot of studies. They do studies with discipline and consistency. This is the professional way for them to train themselves on what they already know, in order to master it, perfect it and **reconnect with the essential element**: the public, their customers.

Keep in mind that the main difference between art and other professional disciplines lies in the quantity and quality of study, training and practice.

You eventually reach a level of artistic training where you realize that knowledge isn't the same thing as learning because you discover that learning involves continuous adjustments and improvements in your way of working.

Providing good care can be emotionally and physically draining because each customer is different, even though they may have similar requirements.

To provide a real good attetion, you have to invest a lot of energy in listening attentively to each customer and in developing the maturity to set aside your ego.

This energy is like gasoline and a good part of it is consumed by day-to-day work routines and customers.

For this reason, daily training on customer care takes on special importance.

As I mentioned at the beginning of this book, continuously refreshing your training prevents you from **underestimating** the basics and from taking anything for qranted.

Constant training in the art of providing customer care is like taking your intelligence to the gym and refilling the emotional tank of your professionalism.

10 | Care to make a positive impact

Art influences people's moods. It can make them feel good or bad. It all depends on the artist's intention and performance.

The same happens when you are a customer care professional. **You are always influencing** the people you attend, whether positively or negatively.

The things you do to help people impact their moods. The things you say to them while you're helping them also play a role. However, sometimes what you don't do or don't say is even more influential.

When it comes to customer service, there is never a moment when you don't influence the people in front of you and around you.

For example, you also make an impact on other customers who are waiting to be helped when they see how you treat the person in front of you.

In customer service, your actions and behavior are much more valuable and significant than your words. So, the most effective way to gauge the quality of your attention is in terms of its positive influence.

That is, you provide good service when you make a conscious effort to positively influence your customers' moods, addressing their needs and requests **with pleasure** and special dedication.

In contrast, your professional performance becomes inferior when you simply worry about your job duties and neglect the people you are supposed to serve. These are the cases in which you exert a negative influence.

Remember, good care is related to your **attitude toward what you do**, which is why you influence customers more through the way you work and help them than through simply performing your duties.

If people don't feel like you have given them good service, it's because you haven't positively influenced their perception of the way you serve them.

11 | Relate to people constructively

This is the basis for making customers feel like they have received good attention after interacting with you.

Relating to people in a constructive way means:

• *Listening to them* in earnest in order to fully understand their needs and circumstances

• *Listening to them* and helping them without judging how they are, how they talk or how they dress

• *Listening to them* attentively in order to identify exactly how you can help them

• *Helping them* in such a way that they can see how much you enjoy doing it and how dignified it makes you feel

• *Acting* with all the diligence that is required in order to help them

Your connection with customers depends on the way you take care of them and react to their needs and requests.

In this case, relating constructively or positively isn't merely a synonym for "sympathy", but instead the type of professionalism that I mentioned in Practice #7.

Your way of **positively relating** to customers also depends on the type of business in which you work and your specific duties.

It's very important that you consider the conditions under which customers come to you and the impact your job makes on their moods.

Working in a clothing store, restaurant or car lot is different from working in a hospital, insurance company or funeral home.

The exact same kind of "sympathy" in each of these jobs could be interpreted in different ways by the customers.

Relating constructively doesn't mean simply agreeing with everything the customer says, but instead means making him or her really sense your desire and commitment to help and the professional dignity and pleasure you derive from doing so.

12 | Customers must matter to you

If they matter to you, you will be able to relate to them. This is the only way to show them that you are interested in their needs and that you want to help them.

When customers come to you and you don't make eye contact with them, don't greet them appropriately, don't welcome them or don't offer your help, their *interpretation* is that they don't matter to you.

This negative feeling can put strain on the relationship and make it hard for customers to feel like they can trust you.

If you don't demonstrate that they matter to you, they will be uncertain about the quality and sincerity of the service you provide.

If you don't look up from the computer, the papers on your desk or your cell phone when a customer is talking to you, you are demonstrating that those other things are more important to you than he or she is.

You make customers feel that they matter to you through your behavior and *specific actions*. For example:

• When you get up to greet them instead of ignoring them until they come to you.

• When you listen to them respectfully without interrupting.

• When you confirm that you have understood them correctly by paraphrasing what they said to you.

If you don't **make them feel** like they are important to you, it's likely that they will reproach you and tell you to stop acting like you're doing them a favor, because they are the ones who are paying for a service and they are the ones who pay your salary.

In comparison, when you feel that serving and helping people is dignified work, it's easy to make them feel like you really value them, both as people and as customers.

When customers **matter to you**, your enthusiasm isn't dampened, but instead you shine with dignity through your actions.

13 | You must feel true appreciation

In order to relate to customers and make a positive impact on them, you must feel true appreciation for them as people.

It is indispensable that you consider them as the **originators** of your job, the reason behind your job duties and the source of your best opportunities for professional growth.

Remember that customers can tell when you are helping them because they matter to you as people and when you are only pretending that they matter to you.

If you fake care, they will feel like you are insincere, both with them and with yourself, and they won't trust you.

Customers know that, when they are **genuinely appreciated**, you will really help them and not just try to brush them off quickly.

Customers know that true appreciation translates into a good attitude when it comes to helping them and collaborating with them.

If you feel true appreciation, you won't be annoyed or bothered when helping them. You won't try to fool them and you will make more of an effort to assist them.

Once you understand the value of customers to your career, you develop the **necessary maturity** to avoid dismissing them or treating them judgmentally.

Truly appreciating customers is one of the most important challenges for customer care professionals. It's not only part of your job; it also means appreciating yourself as a person.

However, **true customer appreciation** is something you decide on. It is a personal matter and you can't feel it out of obligation.

If you provide service simply as one more job duty, you are never going to give your best. You will feel annoyed by your work, and it will be very hard for you to see the opportunities for growth that arise from feeling true appreciation for your customers.

14 | You must be authentic

At one time, it was said that customer service was "performed", and in many companies, they still say this. It's understandable because, in those times, good service was a luxury.

Very few companies believed that good customer service was **a key component** of their business. They simply thought of it as something that could be provided as "value added".

However, the markets have become much more competitive. Some companies started to realize that service levels influenced both the loyalty of their customers and the costs of gaining and keeping their business.

Customers underwent an evolution of their own, becoming aware of the fact that they had power over the fate of companies.

So, there is no doubt that, **if you are faking it** when you help them, it is very likely that they will be upset because you are just reading a script and aren't giving them your best.

When you "perform" customer service, your personality is dulled and you make your customers feel disrespected. If you provide service as "value added", it will seem as if you think you are doing them a favor.

When customer service is "performed", **you limit yourself** to your job description and you stop making the effort to really help people.

Your best only comes out if you enjoy helping customers. You become authentic, genuine, sure-footed, positive, creative and self-respecting.

Customers want the people who help them to give their best because this ensures that they will really receive assistance.

Your positive influence begins with your authenticity, and if you aren't authentic in your appreciation of your customers, you won't be able to relate to them in a constructive way.

Remember, authenticity isn't a customer service technique. Authenticity is made up of the true feelings and **values you have** with regard to your work and yourself as a person.

15 | It involves personal excellence

As you have seen by now, providing people with genuine care is a matter you must take up as **something personal**, which requires a lot of maturity and courage.

Excellence isn't a destination, but rather the road you choose to follow in reaching your goals.

The Greek philosopher, Aristotle, said, "Moral excellence comes about as a result of habit. We become just by doing just acts, temperate by doing temperate acts and brave by doing brave acts".

So, we could say that personal excellence isn't an absolute state, but instead the sum of many actions that have specific characteristics in common.

Your excellence as a person is expressed through your **behavior and attitude** toward customers, toward the work you do, toward learning, continuous improvement and self-motivation, and through what you demand from yourself.

Performing with excellence is performing with a heightened awareness of what it means to be a professional.

Personal excellence is demonstrated in your day-to-day work, including:

• When you do more with less.

• When you give more than what is expected of you.

• When you are authentic in your appreciation of your customers.

• When you practice what you preach.

• When you make a positive impact on the people you help.

• When you are useful and really assist people.

• When you don't worry about what everyone else is going to say.

• When you practice and study to keep yourself motivated.

• When you stop waiting for solutions and, instead, create them and become part of them.

16 | Personal excellence is your decision

Artful customer care goes beyond your work; ***it is a vision*** of yourself, your life and your performance.

It's something you can't do well if you do it unwillingly. No one can force you to serve and work with joy and dignity.

Your willingness to perform with excellence depends on your decision, the ***desire*** you have to do it and your **commitment** to yourself.

So, excellence is your decision. You have the power to decide to give great attetion and not simply provide service that is indifferent or mechanical just "to get it over with".

When you decide to work with excellence, you choose to **make a difference** for yourself and each person you interact with in your work.

This means that you try to give each person you help the experience of being served and appreciated because you realize that your work contributes to improving those people's lives, as well as your own life.

Ultimately, you are who decide the way in which you perform professionally. Remember that boredom isn't a characteristic of a job, but rather the way you have decided to perform that job.

You choose your professional attitude. You won't find this in the procedures manual, the company regulations or your job description.

You are the one who chooses how you work and the one who decides whether or not you enjoy what you do.

You also choose how you wish customers to perceive you and how you wish to influence them.

You are the one who makes *the difference* in the quality of customer care.

Even if you decide not to decide, you are still deciding to postpone things or leave them as they are.

Keep in mind that your decisions are as authentic as you should be in your work.

17 | Care is what you make people feel

When it comes to customers, many people refer to "attention" as if it were the same thing as "service". I mentioned this at the beginning of this book, but I really want to emphasize the differences, as this is a key aspect of providing good customer care.

Customer service consists of what you give them or say to them. But when I speak of "attention", I am referring to feel what you do to people you serve.

This principle explains why customers are dissatisfied or upset when you serve them adequately but give them poor attention.

For example, you can give a customer the correct information, but if you appear annoyed, he or she will always remember your bad attitude more than the good information.

Customers can forget what you tell them or give them, but they won't forget how you make them feel through the way you attend them.

Both the company you work for and you provide a service, but the **quality of care** is 100% in your hands. It is your decision.

The way in which you assist a customer is what demonstrates whether you really want to help or not and how you feel about the work you do.

So, in order to prevent customers from feeling like they have received poor attention:

• Don't treat them indifferently or coldly.

• Don't help them as if you are trying to "brush them off" quickly.

• Don't behave mechanically, "lifelessly" or as if you were a robot.

• Don't justify not being able to help them because of what it says in "the manual" or "the regulations".

• Don't dismiss them because of their appearance, their opinions or their customs.

• Don't make promises you can't keep.

• Don't disrespect their time by being vague about when you're going to help them.

• Don't blame your coworkers or other departments for mistakes.

18 | Get in the habit of asking questions

The most efficient way **to determine** the true needs of customers is by asking them what they want, what they need, what you can do for them and how you can help them.

If you don't ask, you end up making assumptions or guessing. In customer service, don't assume anything or take anything for granted: ask.

When you provide service based on your **assumptions**, you run the risk of offending customers because this tells them that your opinion matters more than theirs.

Gone are the days of the Golden Rule of Customer Service ("Treat customers the way you would like to be treated") and the Platinum Rule ("Don't give your customers what you would like because they may want something different"). **Asking is more efficient** than either of these rules.

Professionalism in customer service is based on your ability to ask questions. That is the only way you can create solutions that are personalized for each customer.

Ask questions to **investigate** and identify the best way you can help. When you ask questions, you open the flood gates of opportunity and make the customer feel like you are genuinely interested in helping him or her.

Learning to **interview** customers is a creative habit you must cultivate in order to achieve a broader vision of their concerns, needs and requests.

Questions are the means, but the end is to **generate responses**. The primary objective is to understand what customers are really seeking so that you can act with diligence.

Asking questions is also a strategic communication exercise for stimulating customers to reveal the key necessities that need to be satisfied.

Keep in mind that people who don't ask questions always risk more than those who do.

19 | Listen "between the lines"

Customers always know what they need and what they don't need, but at times, they express this to you in ways that are unclear.

Sometimes it isn't enough just to listen to them attentively. Instead, you also have to further **investigate** what they're really trying to tell you.

The key to understanding them involves paying attention **without judging** or discrediting them. Only then you can listen "between the lines" and pick up on their less obvious concerns.

If you label them, it will be very hard to understand what they really need.

Sometimes one question isn't enough and you have to **interview them** with direct questions. For example:

—What do you need specifically?

—What is the issue you want to resolve?

—What do plan to use this product for?

—What concerns you most about the product?

In more complex situations, it might be a good strategy to **paraphrase**. This is an efficient, professional way to **verify** that you have correctly understood what the customer is trying to say.

To paraphrase means to repeat the customer's statements or questions in your own words.

For example, you can begin by saying something like: "Let me see if I have understood you correctly. What you are looking for is...".

When you paraphrase, you **make customers feel** like:

• It is very important to you to understand them so that you can provide good service.

• It isn't an annoyance for you to help them and focus on them.

• You are responsible and diligent in your work.

• You like helping people and you have **cultivated** the necessary patience to do it with supreme artistry.

20 | Offer options and alternatives

Customers don't like being "boxed in" or put up **against a wall**. They feel like they are being treated this way when they are told, "This is the only product we have left", "This is all we have", or "We don't have that right now".

If you are a true customer service professional, you have learned to present alternative options and solutions for their requests: "We don't have that product, but we do have this one", "We don't have it right now, but we will have it in X amount of time", or "Let me find out where I can get it for you".

Customers want you to offer them options because this reaffirms their freedom and their power to **choose**. They would rather feel like they have a choice than feel like they have to accept the one, single solution you offer.

Help them decide between various alternatives, happily explaining the benefits of each one so it will be easier to compare them and determine their value.

When you offer them more than one option in products, services or solutions, customers are captivated because they realize that you like helping them choose the best one.

Creating options for customers isn't more work, but rather a different kind of creative effort, which fuels the development of your professionalism.

Of course, you can only create alternatives when you focus on helping people and have a thorough understanding of the scope of your work and the details of the company you represent.

If you're content to limit yourself to "yes" or "no" answers, it is hard to provide your customers with good service, to help them or to offer them options.

If what you do is annoying to you, and you don't like assisting customers, it is very unlikely that you will look for options to offer them.

In other words, the process of creating options is **beneficial to you** because it empowers your intelligence and your knowledge about the work you do and it stimulates your creativity.

When you offer customers options and alternatives, your professionalism always comes out ahead.

21 | Focus on what you can do

Customers aren't interested in what you **can't** do or what you **don't** have. When your responses are limited to that, they feel as if you are ignoring them or providing them with poor service.

Don't structure **your responses** on the basis of "I don't have...", "There isn't any...", "This product hasn't come in yet", "I can't...", "We don't provide that service", "We can't do that", or "Unfortunately, we can't".

If you focus on helping customers using the means at your disposal, your responses will be geared toward offering **options and alternative solutions** and will be more along the lines of:

—We don't have that service (or product) but we do have the following ones that do the same thing or something similar...

—That product hasn't come in yet, but:
 -We have this other brand...
 -We'll have it next week...
 -If you give me your number, I'll call you when it arrives...

—Let's call the purchasing department (or our vendor) right now to find out when we're going to receive it...

—I can't help you right now, but...
  -As soon as I finish helping this other person, I'll be with you.
  -As soon as I finish this call, I'm all yours.

If you focus on what you can do and what's within your reach, you will discover a great source of opportunities for professional and personal growth.

When you focus on what you can do, you realize the immense *potential* you have that perhaps you haven't fully utilized.

As you can see, by focusing on what you can do, in one way or another, you are also focusing on increasing your possibilities for professional and personal *growth*.

Thinking about what you can do for the customer and focusing on that will lead you to discover that you can always help and provide good service.

22 | Be an ambassador

Customer service professionals are essentially:

• Ambassadors of their feelings about themselves and their work.

• Ambassadors of the company they work for.

• Ambassadors of the products and services they represent.

• Ambassadors of their coworkers, both from the same department and from all the other departments.

Ambassadors are representatives of the people of a country, their culture and their way of life. This is what customers expect from you when you assist them.

When you are in front of them, you are the face of all the people who make up your company; **you personify the company** you work for.

If you don't act like a good ambassador, you will never be able to provide good service and will never be able to perform your work with dignity.

If you don't act like an ambassador, your customers will feel that your job annoys you, that it bores you to help them and that you aren't interested in being useful.

The best ambassadors **face** their customers and clearly demonstrate the pride they take in their company, even if the customer's needs end up being met by another department or another person.

Good customer service ambassadors don't criticize anyone in their company in order to justify a mistake to their customers.

When you are a good ambassador, you understand that you **are always part** of the process of meeting customers' needs, and this is why you focus on helping them and going with them wherever they need to go to satisfy those needs.

Poor ambassadors "bounce" customers around and blame others for mistakes or poor service.

Good ambassadors know that customers aren't looking for someone to blame, but instead are looking for assistance and artful care.

23 | Don't "bounce" customers around

"Bouncing" customers around is **evading** them, avoiding them, dodging them, **brushing them off** or dismissing them with excuses for not helping them.

If you make customers go from one department to another without helping them or responding to their requests, you are bouncing them around.

If customers need guidance on a product or service, **give them** all the necessary information. Explain all the requirements to them at once and show them everything they must do.

When you give customers incomplete information, you waste their time unnecessarily by forcing them to come back again and again.

Remember that, to customers, you are the company you work for, you are its representative and **you are its ambassador**.

If you tell customers that their issues can't be handled by you or your department or can't be addressed at that time, they already know that you are going to bounce them around because you aren't really interested in helping them.

When you bounce customers around, you simply **postpone** the response, the solution or the help they are seeking; as a consequence:

1. You run the risk of them coming back to you accompanied by your boss.

2. You risk losing the customer, the trust of your coworkers and your credibility with your boss.

3. You risk being a bad employee and losing your job.

The consequences of bouncing customers around are as simple as that.

Bouncing customers around shows a lack of professionalism and is an act of **cruelty**: There are people who purposely provide incomplete information, make up requirements or transfer customers to the wrong departments.

Remember: not bouncing a customer around is a basic act of **self-respect**.

When you bounce customers around, you are also bouncing yourself around as a professional, including your opportunities for development.

24 | Don't use your coworkers as an excuse

Don't tell customers that you can't help them because the person who's supposed to do it didn't come to work or isn't in at the time.

Don't "**bounce**" customers around with that excuse.

Remember that, in those situations, you can provide good service by:

1. **Listening** to the customer in order to understand his or her situation

2. **Making a note** of the issue, including the customer's name, telephone number and other relevant information, so that you can precisely inform the coworker who will be responsible for resolving the issue

3. **Promising** the customer that you will inform the appropriate person or department and that you will follow up on the matter

If you use your coworkers' failings as an excuse for not providing care, your customers will know that you are simply **evading them**.

Another thing to avoid is telling customers that a service error occurred because the person who helped them was new, poorly-trained or just careless.

When you badmouth your coworkers in front of customers, you never come out looking good because it shows your lack of ambassadorship and professionalism.

Far from exonerating yourself, when you blame poor service on the people you work with, customers feel that, if you can't be loyal to your coworkers, it's unlikely that you will be loyal to them.

Blaming your coworkers in front of customers doesn't make them look bad; it makes you look bad.

Discretion is a virtue in front of customers, and there is a saying that sums up the matter concisely: "Don't air your dirty laundry".

Review Practice #22: Be an ambassador.

25 | Care for your internal customers

Your coworkers and your providers at every level and in every area are your internal customers. They are part of your permanent **team**, and as such, you also owe them artful, supreme attention.

However, the quality of the relationship you establish with your internal customers is determined by how you perceive them.

If you appreciate them as customers, you will do your best to **understand and satisfy** their needs. That is, you will treat them better when you consider them as customers.

Now, if you don't take good care of the people with whom you spend the greater part of your workday, you can be sure that your external customers will sense a significant degree of professional inconsistency on your part. The reason is simple: it's very hard to treat your external customers well if you don't first treat your internal customers well.

A **vision** of your coworkers as internal customers motivates you to take care of them in a special way, listening to them with more respect, being more careful how you communicate with them, having more patience with them and trying to better understand the reasons behind their requests in order to better satisfy them. You become aware that you share a professional **commitment** to customer service with them.

Besides, if you treat your providers like internal customers, you will obtain better products and services from them because that perspective compels you to devote more strategic care to your **relationship** with them.

If you treat them only with regard to the duties they have to you or your company, you will never receive their full sincerity, commitment or loyalty.

Thinking of coworkers and providers as internal customers doesn't mean demanding less from them or letting their mistakes slide by. On the contrary, it means understanding that your relationship with them requires more effort because you have a **long-term daily connection** with them. A good part of your work depends on their work.

If you cultivate supreme artistry in your relationship with your internal customers, you build the necessary trust for dealing with errors with maturity and professionalism so that they can be corrected without jeopardizing the relationship.

26 | Teamwork is your responsibility

Customers evaluate service based on the **worst performance**.

Let me explain this key principle by using a restaurant as an example:

The food and the service provided by the whole staff may be good, but if you go to the restroom and it's dirty, the quality of the rest of the restaurant's services loses value and you probably won't want to come back.

This example shows how your coworkers can affect the **evaluation of your performance** and why it is so important to work with them as a team.

Don't expect teamwork to be a natural consequence of working at the same company or in the same department. Teamwork is the result of **your decision to join forces** in order to help customers.

Customers know that those people who have a greater sense of teamwork are the ones who provide better service. They know that those people are professional enough to treat their coworkers like internal customers.

Teamwork depends on your individual responsibility and will. It is a result of being mature enough to set aside your ego and ask for help.

Rather than "bouncing" a customer around when he or she requests something that isn't part of your direct job duties, you have an opportunity to demonstrate your professional decision to work as a team by ***asking for help*** from your coworkers.

It's likely that sometimes certain coworkers won't have the same commitment to good service as you do. However, in most cases, this is only the result of not having treated them like internal customers, applying the same principles we have already discussed in this book.

Part of the challenge of artful customer care is having ***the same dedication*** toward coworkers and providers as you do toward external customers. Otherwise, you are being inconsistent.

Also, when you focus on working as a team with less "refined" coworkers, you mature as a person and you empower your creativity.

27 | Understand the scope of your promises

Keep in mind that customers pay for the **promises of benefits** that your company has made to them regarding its products and services. Those promises form **the basis** of the commercial relationship. They are a commitment, an obligation.

Besides expecting the product or service to work the way it's supposed to, customers also expect fulfillment of **basic promises of service** simply for being human beings: they want to be treated with respect, courtesy and sincerity.

These basic promises are inherent in your job as a customer service professional. They are your duty and your responsibility.

However, these promises aren't always fulfilled, which causes customers' **trust** to become fragile and vulnerable. It's a logical response after being disappointed numerous times.

When you feel that the customer in front of you has **preconceived ideas**, resulting in skepticism and distrust, don't judge or reproach him or her for this attitude.

Understand that the customers you perceive as distrustful have surely **been defrauded on many occasions** by other people and companies. When they are in front of you, they feel that there is a latent risk that promises will be broken once more, and this won't come as a surprise to them.

If some of your customers don't clearly perceive your respect, courtesy and sincerity, it is very likely that they will treat you with suspicion and misgivings.

However, if you provide them with good service in the spirit of professionalism and dignity that we have already discussed, you can positively influence their prejudices, earning credibility and trust.

If you **avoid making promises you can't keep**, even little ones, this represents a basic gesture of respect for the customer and for yourself.

One of your most significant professional challenges in providing good customer care is precisely that: earning and maintaining the confidence and trust of your customers. This is why it is essential for you to understand the significance of your promises.

28 | Respect your customers' time

This is part of the **basic respect** that customers expect from you and the company you work for.

You are disrespecting their time when you promise that you are going to fulfill their needs or requests within a given timeframe and then don't do it.

You can be sure that **they will feel disrespected** if you tell them that what you have to do will only take "a second" or "a minute" and then it ends up taking a half-hour or more.

However, telling them that you don't know how long it will take to resolve their request isn't the answer, either.

If you are an excellent customer service professional, you have already handled thousands of similar situations and you have a certain sense of how much time it will take. So, give them that information.

Let customers know how much time it will take to handle their requests and make them feel like they have the right to decide to wait rather than feeling like you are "obligating" them to wait (review Practice #20 on the importance of offering options).

It is fitting to add that there are many myths about how "hurried" customers are. It isn't true that they are always in a hurry. Most of the time, customers are willing to wait for a service, but it is something that **they want to decide** for themselves.

If they come to a place of business where no one welcomes them, greets them appropriately, makes eye contact or offers to help them, customers immediately become **wary** of how long it will take for someone to help them and **prejudiced** against the people who finally do.

Likewise, it is an act of respect for your customers if you suggest that they can take care of other errands rather than having to wait there while you handle their request or if you tell them that you will call them at a given time once their request has been fulfilled.

Don't tell them that managing their request will take "a little while", "just a moment" or "a long time" because these are very ambiguous expressions. Be an informed professional and offer an estimated time that is as **precise as possible**. The customers will feel more respected, valued and appreciated and will also feel that you are very knowledgeable about your work.

29 | Become "obsessed" with details

Customers are fascinated when you are "obsessive" detail-oriented while helping them, providing information and making them feel welcome in your workplace.

Through your efforts, they will recognize that you are a first-rate professional, you are up to date with your work, you enjoy helping people and you are a specialist in your field.

Being "obsessive" with your customers **signifies** always demonstrating a **tendency** toward initiative, foresight, tenacity and consistency in the details of the process of helping and serving them.

When you are an obsessively detail-oriented professional, you focus on anticipating or exceeding customers' expectations, giving them even more than they hoped for.

The following behaviors are examples of "obsession" with details in order to **anticipate** customers' needs or **exceed** their expectations:

• You don't only arrive on time, but arrive a little early.

• You don't wait for customers to call you about a pending matter: you call them first.

• You don't wait for a customer's service to expire, but instead you help him or her renew it far enough in advance to avoid any potential trouble.

• Your update, record and organize your customer requests so you won't forget about any of them once the customer is ready.

• You offer customers options and alternative solutions to their needs.

• You give them detailed information about the amount of time it will take to resolve their issues.

• You get up from your desk and go to greet the customer instead of waiting for him or her to come to you.

• You make eye contact with the customer and greet him or her from a few yards away.

Lastly, you are "obsessed" with details when you surprise customers by giving them much more attention than they were expecting from you and when you don't wait for them to follow up on their requests. Put simply, you are always a step ahead of them in order to give them the best possible service.

30 | Address complaints with professionalism

First of all, you must understand **the origin** of customer claims or complaints:

1. They feel that they **didn't receive** the quality of service or product that they paid for (broken promises). For this reason, they feel like they have been duped.

2. They feel like they **have been treated** unfairly or disrespectfully. For example, they were "bounced around", their time wasn't respected, they were ignored, no one listened to them, no one made eye contact or they weren't made to feel welcome.

Customers who feel like they have been deceived or disrespected have good reason to be angry and to express their disappointment without special considerations. So, the way in which customers express their anger, deception or frustration is something that shouldn't affect your professionalism when handling a claim.

A customer service professional **doesn't spend even a second judging** whether the customer is justified or not or whether the claim is being presented in a rude way or not. The customer isn't being rude to you, but instead to the company that has treated him or her rudely by not keeping its promises.

Also remember that, in customer service, all of the workers at a company are **ambassadors**, and customers can only present their claims to the company's ambassadors, meaning you. So, their complaints aren't personally directed at you.

Don't blame coworkers or other departments or try to justify yourself by saying that you don't have the authority to do something to help a customer.

Don't blame external factors, either (for example, "The administrative software isn't working correctly") because, from a customer's point of view, these are just excuses for poor service, and that will make him or her even more angry.

Handling claims professionally implies having the necessary **personal maturity** to focus on the content, the background and the significance of the claim.

Only from this standpoint can you perform with supreme artistry and **use your full intelligence** to help the customer. Otherwise, you will end up confronting him or her and initiating a vicious circle of discontent.

31 | Don't "educate" your customers

If we aren't customer service professionals, we tend to think that, if people are rude or bad-mannered when presenting a complaint or claim, they "need to be put in their place".

This notion reflects:

• Lack of understanding of the origins of customer complaints.

• Lack of knowledge about how to manage these situations professionally.

Your job is to **serve and help** customers, not to try to change their personalities.

In situations where customers are very upset because of the poor quality of a product, a service or the assistance they received before they came to you and they express themselves in a discourteous way, your main job is to **understand the origin of their anger** and not to judge the spirit in which they express their discontent.

If you focus on judging customers' personalities, behavior or "bad manners" at that moment, you will lose focus, leading to a bitter and fruitless conversation.

If customers feel deceived or mistreated by you, a coworker or the company, **it doesn't make sense** for you to expect them to be polite. Whether or not they are right to be "so" upset, you're going to clear things up after you handle their complaint with professionalism (before that time, it won't do you any good).

While these upset customers are rudely expressing their disappointment, **don't interrupt them** telling them to lower their voice or stop yelling at you or saying that they have bad manners. That will only make the situation worse.

In those cases, customers won't feel like you are helping, but instead that you feel superior to them, and that's why you dare to interrupt them and demand respect. They will become even more combative to defend their pride.

It could be that the person usually has very good manners and you simply don't know exactly what happened with regard to the service he or she received that was **the straw that broke the camel's back**.

Remember, customer discontent stems from feeling disrespected and mistreated by your company, and you are its **ambassador** (their best option for getting help).

32 | Don't argue with angry customers

Dealing with angry customers is the ultimate test of your professionalism because it is the moment when your true abilities in this area are most exposed.

Whatever the reason behind customers' discontent, I propose the following five essential steps for providing good service:

1. Let them vent and don't interrupt them. Listen to them attentively with respect and earnestness. There are two advantages to listening this way:

First: The more they express their anger, the better they will feel in the end.

Second: You will have more time to think and demonstrate your emotional maturity in response to their anger.

Don't waste one second judging customers. Just focus on the background information and resist the (understandable) temptation to run away from the situation. You will only postpone any resolution and make the customers feel worse than they already do.

2. When they finish talking, apologize. This can be very difficult because you may feel like it's unfair. However, apologizing doesn't mean that you are accepting the blame for a mistake or rude service. What it really means is that you're sorry that the customer feels upset, whether it's justified or not.

3. Confirm that you have understood and show that you have really listened. Paraphrase customers' complaints by saying, "Please let me see if I have understood you correctly", and then put the reasons for their discontent in your own words.

4. Immediately afterwards, make it clear that you are going to help. Explain what you are going to do in detail. If necessary, also explain in detail the processes and the time involved in resolving the matter. This lets customers know that you care and that you are really going to help them.

5. At the end of the process, apologize again for any inconvenience, thank the customers for the opportunity to assist them and ask if they need anything else. For example, "Is there anything else I can do to help you?"

If they are treated with this kind of professionalism, in 99% of cases, customers will end up very satisfied and will apologize to you for the rude way they expressed their anger initially.

33 | Appreciate the value of complaints

Most of the time, customers who are unhappy because of poor service or attention don't say anything. Instead, they get revenge in two ways: they don't come back, and whenever they can, they badmouth you and your company.

So, **when they do complain, they are giving you the opportunity** to prevent them from taking their business elsewhere and tarnishing your company's image and reputation.

Of course, an angry person's complaint isn't a pleasant thing. If you feel attacked, insulted or provoked, it's only human to want to run away from the situation. You will want to escape from this unpleasant scenario as quickly as possible with as little discomfort as possible or else you will want to fight in order to get even and "restore" your honor.

In both cases, **listening and handling complaints** with professionalism and efficacy depends on your maturity as a person and your ability to understand that what's at stake isn't your ego or your pride, but your professionalism.

In customer care, your job isn't to put "complainers" in their place, but to understand the origins of their anger so that you can really help them with supreme artistry and make your relationship with them fruitful.

Listen to them to understand what they expect and why they are disappointed.

This information is extremely important because it is the true origin of the complaint. It could also be an **opportunity to anticipate** future mistakes and correct them or to make significant improvements in the products and services offered by your company.

Additionally, keep in mind two aspects of the strategic value of complaints:

1. Many companies pay for costly market research to find out why customers are dissatisfied. So, when they complain directly to you, they are providing valuable information for free, saving you a lot of money.

2. Customers complain because they want you and your company to improve so they can continue being your customers. When you don't matter to them anymore, they simply stop complaining and take their business to one of your competitors. It's that simple. That's why it is so important for you to value customer complaints.

34 "Stimulate" complaints

If customers' complaints are an indication of their desire for you to improve so they can continue being your customers, then, stimulating complaints is a **very valuable** undertaking, even though it may seem counterproductive (especially if you believe that an absence of complaints means that service is always good).

Keep in mind that most customers who feel that they received poor care aren't going to say anything. If you didn't give them good service, they tend to think, "Why should I waste my time with you?"

Furthermore, if you don't stimulate complaints, they will always come in an "explosive" way, like turning on a faucet that hasn't been used in a long time. However, when you have a **plan for eliciting comments** from customers and channeling them immediately, the complaints lose their aggressive tone and become suggestions and opportunities for improvement.

To strategically stimulate comments, you must be proactive and courageous enough to ask direct questions, like: "What could I do better the next time you come?" or "What improvements would you like to see in our products and services?"

As you can see, these questions are very different from: "What did you think about the service?" or "What's your opinion of this product?" These questions are very **vague**, and it would be easy for an unhappy customer to dismiss them or save time by simply responding, "It was fine".

If you want to receive valuable suggestions, you must refer to very specific aspects in your questions and be insistent. Even if a customer is satisfied, there will almost always be something he or she thinks could be better the next time.

By stimulating complaints, *your goal is to obtain responses* that will help you:

1. Learn about customers' needs and dissatisfaction immediately at no additional cost.

2. Identify recurring errors and faults that can be definitively resolved.

3. Proactively seek opportunities for improvement or for the creation of new products and services.

4. Build your customers' trust and loyalty.

35 | React artfully in the event of mistakes

Customers don't expect that your company's products and services will always be perfect or that there will never be mistakes. They don't expect that of you, either. They *are willing to accept and forgive* those failings if you react professionally when they occur.

Customers do legitimately expect you to keep all your promises (Practice #27), to respect their time (Practice #28), to be "obsessive" about details (Practice #29), to handle their complaints professionally (Practice #30) and to react artfully in the event of mistakes on your part (Practice #35).

At the highest levels of artful performance, there is a keen awareness of these aspects. It is understood that, at any given moment, it doesn't make sense to hide a mistake from the public. What does make sense is *being prepared* to react professionally when mistakes happen.

If you are assisting a customer and have to carry out various other activities at the same time, you might not give that person 100% of your attention, but he or she *will be 100% focused* on everything you're doing, down to the tiniest gesture. That's why, when there is an error and you try to hide it, that's exactly when the customer will notice it the most.

This act of concealment makes the customer **suspicious** of your intentions and your honesty. It would be easy for him or her to wonder, "What are you hiding and why?"

As for artists, they have an overall sense of their work and have identified their most common failings and the risks of these occurring. This is why they have a corresponding action plan.

High-level artists don't spend time trying to **conceal things**. They are prepared and know what to do when an error occurs, which makes their reaction more secure and honest.

To customers, **the way you react** to errors or complaints can end up mattering more than the errors, themselves.

In other words, your attitude in the face of difficulties reveals your true professionalism in customer care and shows your maturity as a person.

36 | Be mindful of your non-verbal communication

Be aware of all the messages you send to customers *without saying* a word.

When you are face-to-face with a customer, what you say by the way you sit and walk, or with your eyes and your tone of voice *can matter* more than your words.

Your non-verbal communication is made up of your facial expressions, gestures and every aspect of your way of speaking, all of which *reflect* your true intentions, feelings, desires thoughts and moods.

Saying "good afternoon" isn't enough. If you are doing it simply because it's a protocol, you could seem like a robot.

If you walk or move in slow motion while handling a customer emergency, to the customer, this means that you *are annoyed* that you have to help him or her.

If you don't look customers in the eyes, they might feel like you don't value them enough, that they aren't welcome or that you simply don't want to help them. **Eye contact shows** interest, presence and a sense of responsibility. If you talk to them while looking the other way, looking at papers or looking at someone else, they could feel ignored and disrespected.

If your body language doesn't match your words, **people can "hear" what you AREN'T saying**.

Your body always sends signals about your willingness and attitude toward real care. For example, if you lean forward a little, this says to the customer, "Tell me more". However, if you lean back too much, you could make him or her feel like you're starting to lose interest.

Sit and walk straight so that you communicate that you are alert and enthusiastic. If you sit back in your chair or lean against the wall, you communicate the opposite and you inspire very little confidence and trust.

The customer **uses** your non-verbal communication **to evaluate** how you really feel about your work and about him or her.

37 | Improve your service over the phone

When people say, "I can't work on the phone", it's because they don't understand the importance of this tool and haven't received training on how to use it professionally.

Customers call you uninformed, worried, confused, dissatisfied or angry, hoping that you'll help them. It's harder than when you're face-to-face because you only have your voice to compensate for the lack of eye contact.

The **non-verbal aspects of telephone communication** that impact customers the most, and which you must be very aware of when helping them through this medium are:

1. Inflection and emphasis: Raising and lowering the pitch and volume of your voice at the beginning, in the middle or at the end of sentences makes it sound less robotic, flat, cold or indifferent.

2. Emotional intensity: The amount of energy you transmit when speaking demonstrates your mood and your level of desire to help customers.

3. Speed: If you speak very quickly, it's hard for customers to understand you and they might think that you're in a hurry to get rid of them. However, if you speak very slowly, they could interpret it as laziness or annoyance at having to help them. You must adapt to the speed at which your customers speak.

4. Rhythm: The order of your words and phrases and the pauses between them show that you are really focused on your conversation and not distracted by something else. Rhythm also refers to the monotonous, repetitive cadence one adopts when speaking with annoyance, tedium or irritation.

5. Volume: Along with the above aspects, the volume of your voice communicates information about your mood, your patience, your stress level and your emotional balance in your work.

6. Breathing: You give customers an opportunity to breathe and let them know that you're there when, during pauses, you interject phrases like: "I understand" or "of course". Otherwise, they might think that you are distracted or aren't listening attentively.

7. Mood: When you feel dignity and pleasure in helping customers, the muscles of your face relax and your voice becomes clearer, stronger and more agreeable. People can tell whether or not you are helping them with supreme artistry.

38 | Best practices over the phone

To improve and maintain your customer care abilities over the phone:

* Periodically **record** some of your calls and listen to yourself. This will enable you to evaluate how you use your voice according to Practice #37. You will also be able to detect possible "pet words and phrases".

* Frequently **change** the outgoing message on your cell phone and office voice-mail. This will help you refresh your image.

* If you are attending a long meeting or a course, say so in your **voice-mail message** and state how long you will be gone and when you will return your calls. You will be surprised by how professional this sounds to customers when they hear it.

* **Review** pending matters at the beginning of the day so that you won't be surprised when you receive calls concerning them. Remember to be "obsessed" with details (Practice #29).

* When you transfer calls, provide the person you are transferring them to with the customer's name and all the details of the matter to be handled so the customer won't

have to **repeat** the whole story when he or she talks to that person.

* **Check** your voice-mail with pencil in hand to write down the details. That way you can return your calls in a more organized fashion.

* Take messages in writing without exceptions. You will save a lot of time. Make sure you note the key information about the person who is calling: his or her name, company, telephone number, email address, cell number and reason for the call. If for some reason you don't hear well, ask him or her to repeat the information, and if necessary, confirm that you have understood correctly.

* At the end of a call, **thank** the customer for his or her time and wait for him or her to hang up first. That way you avoid cutting the customer off.

* Besides creating a harmonious framework in which to better influence the people you talk to, when you smile while talking on the phone, your face relaxes, you can concentrate better, your soft palate widens and your voice takes on more clarity and energy.

39 | Customer care through "virtual" media

I am referring to email, text messages, web pages and social networking sites. All of these are the virtual media of customer care that have gained vital importance in many types of work.

Keep in mind that communicating well and providing **good customer service in writing** can be more difficult than doing it face-to-face or over the phone.

Your customers won't always interpret what you write the way you intended it, as it is hard for a written message to incorporate the non-verbal cues of oral communication.

If you transmit certain messages in writing, you risk being misinterpreted. In that regard, **it isn't recommendable** to argue with customers or make clarifications in writing. In those cases, a phone call or personal meeting is preferable. You can put the agreements in writing afterwards, if necessary. You will save a lot of time and will protect your personal reputation.

If you have no choice but to make clarifications in writing, **don't copy** the message to anyone else. This way the customer can rest assured that you aren't involving other people or trying to cover your back. Written conversations involving other people tend to unleash interminable, unproductive exchanges of messages. If you need to notify another person about the case, it's preferable to do so in a separate message.

Don't **automatically assume** that writing or written notifications are the same thing as communication. There are a number of things that can happen that could prevent customers from realizing that you have written to them or prevent them from accessing your message.

In many cases, it's better to call **before writing**, especially in the event of emergencies, delicate situations or matters that require immediate attention.

As a general rule, keep in mind that every written message in customer service is a **formal public document**, signifying a commitment on your part and that of the company you represent. What you say verbally doesn't end up being stored electronically, but what you write does.

To explore this topic in depth, I recommend that you consult my book, "Email at the Workplace" (http://tinyurl.com/4jte3w).

40 | Don't "label" customers

By "labels" I am referring to the extensive variety of **qualifying adjectives** we apply to customers and get "hung up" on. Examples include: "annoying customer", "difficult", "foulmouthed", "liar", "deadbeat", "ungrateful" or "rude".

Labels function as a sort of qualifier we use to **pigeonhole** people and situations according to a single personality trait, behavior or circumstance at a given moment.

When you label a person, you **condemn** him or her to being perceived exclusively in that way with an apparent inability to change. Worse yet, you condemn yourself to believing that you can't do anything to influence positively that person (I believe that it would be worthwhile to review Practice #10).

We all label people and are labeled by them throughout our lives. It has become a sort of habit. However, the **consequences** in customer care are always **negative**:

1. Labels cause your communications to be based on prejudices, which diminishes your creativity in providing good service.

2. Labels function as a **barrier** that makes it harder for you to see other qualities or virtues in people and situations.

3. Labels **hinder you** from identifying other options or alternative solutions to customers' requests and needs.

Labels make you inflexible, and the negative effects are so strong that even "positive" labels can be harmful. For example, if you label a customer as "calm", the day he or she is dissatisfied or disgruntled by your service, you will be caught off guard.

Many times poor service originates from a **lack of the necessary professional maturity** to avoid labeling a customer.

We label people **unconsciously**. This is why it may be useful to have another person help you by alerting you any time you are "blocked" with regard to a customer or situation because you are "hung up" on a label.

Labels **drain** your creative ability to confront challenges and grow as a person.

41 | Use policies to help

Don't use company policies, manuals and regulations as an excuse not to provide customers with good service.

Customers feel very **frustrated** when you quote regulations in order to justify why you "can't do anything about it". Remember that you can always help them (review Practice #4).

Customers don't care about what you can't do. This is why they become disillusioned when you tell them:

* "Unfortunately, we can't do that..."

* "That isn't our policy..."

* "The company regulations prevent me from doing that..."

* "This department doesn't handle that and it's not my job..."

* "I would really like to help you, but I can't..."

Companies establish regulations **for purposes of ensuring** that customers receive excellent products and high-quality services.

It would be very strange and a major cause for concern if there were regulations in your company that prohibited good care, full service or helping customers (I believe that this would be a good time to review Practice #3 and #21).

If you are an excellent customer care professional, you must conscientiously **study** the origins and true scope of your company's written regulations (if any) in such a way that you can use them to help your customers. Otherwise, you will end up repeating supposed prohibitions like a parrot.

Utilizing your company's manuals or regulations as **a guide for providing excellent care** is a challenge to your intelligence and creativity.

Don't use them mechanically, as if you were a robot, or simply to "brush off" customers and get rid of them quickly. If you do, you will only end up turning your relationship with your customers into something unpleasant and professionally frustrating.

42 | Stop greeting people mechanically

In customer care, a greeting is the **fundamental initial connection**, which affects and determines where the interaction process will lead. It's that important.

Many people greet customers mechanically with questions like: "How are you?" "How's it going?" or "How have you been?" Most of the time they only do it as a formality and the response doesn't really matter to them. They greet people automatically, without being aware of the value of a greeting for human interactions.

Although it may seem inconsequential, a greeting reveals your mood and your true feelings about the person you are receiving.

Furthermore, a greeting satisfies the basic need to be acknowledged. This is why our mood is negatively affected when we are ignored by the people whose services we need.

Customer care professionals are conscious of how mechanized the act of greeting has become. This is why they don't greet customers with questions about how they are, but instead with expressions that **make them feel** welcome and let them know that they will be assisted with pleasure and not annoyance.

"Good afternoon. Welcome! Thank you for stopping by. Come on in". This is a good example of a different kind of greeting that is geared toward making a **positive impact** on the person you are going to help.

When you simply say: "How are you?" or "How's it going?" you are repeating generic expressions that are used **routinely**.

People receiving a routine greeting won't feel like you are happy to see them or help them, but instead that you are simply greeting them out of convention like an automaton.

When you become a customer care artist, you must be aware of the opportunity your greeting gives you to **establish interaction** with people.

With the appropriate greeting, you can make them feel that you are alert and awake, that it's your pleasure to help them, that you are "obsessive" about details and that you are making a conscious effort to make them feel welcome in your workplace.

Giving a cordial, authentic and different greeting to each customer is one of the most important professional challenges because it forces you to focus on people (please review Practice #11).

43 | Change the way you greet people

Greeting people in different ways gives you the **opportunity to become more animated** and to pleasantly surprise your customers.

When you change your greeting, you resume control of your communicative abilities and you acquire more energy for initiating the process of serving the next customer.

That is, changing your greeting is a strategy for **saving yourself** from the chronically mechanized behavior that leads to unconscious work routines.

There are greetings that more clearly **communicate** pleasure in helping people and that are differentiated from the stereotypical questions: "How are you?" and "How's it going?" The following are just a few examples of alternative greetings:

—"Hi! It's so nice to see you!"

—"Good afternoon. Thank you for coming. How can I help you?"

—"Welcome! Come in!"

—"We're so happy to see you again! Thank you for stopping by!"

—"Hi! Welcome! We're glad you're here!"

—"Thank you for coming back. Come in! We're happy to see you!"

It's likely that, when you first change your greeting, these phrases perhaps will feel "unnatural" to you. And it would be hard to feel natural if you have greeted people with the same **routine questions** all your life. However, you can be sure that, with practice, they will become more spontaneous and productive.

Use the above examples of greetings as a point of departure. Later on, you can invent your own combinations and **create your own greetings** to fit different customers, moments and situations.

The goal of changing your greeting is to stop doing it mechanically and lifelessly, as if it required a lot of effort on your part.

Change your greeting to give yourself an opportunity to **reconnect** with the best part of yourself. Stop greeting people just for the sake of greeting them. Greet the people you are about to help to influence them and make a difference to them.

44 | Use the customer's name constantly

People's names are an essential part of their **identity**. This is why addressing someone by name can make a big difference in any interpersonal communication process.

Using your customers' names is a high-level professional practice because it means that you are **focused** on them as people.

Otherwise, you will simply treat them like numbers, invoices, budgets, collection accounts, pending matters, complaints or "problems". These are nothing but labels (see Practice #40).

You have **greater influence** when you treat people like human beings. When you address them by name, it's like music to their ears because they feel like you are really paying attention them, that you respect them and appreciate them, and that it doesn't annoy you to help them.

So, if you know their names, please use them. If you need to see their identification or credit card for some reason, take advantage of the opportunity to make a mental note of their name so you can start using it.

If you don't know their name, greet them, introduce yourself and then **ask them**: "Hi! Good afternoon. It's a pleasure to meet you. I'm Juan Carlos Jimenez. What's your name?" Once you know it, use it actively every chance you get.

Knowing and using your customers' names is one of the essential aspects of good customer care that is most underutilized in practice. It's very likely that unconscious work routines will lead you to forget this important point or take it for granted.

Making the effort to know and use your customers' names is a good antidote to the mechanized attitude that results from day-to-day routines.

It's more than simply a "detail". It's an act of basic **consistency** for customer care professionals at an artistic performance level.

Greeting people appropriately and addressing them by name are two indispensable conditions **for making your work shine** and maintaining a positive connection with your customers.

45 | Get to know your customers better

When you are helping people, the better you know them, the better your chances will be to **positively influence** them (see Practice #10) and provide them with artful attention.

Depending on your specific job duties, you may have more or fewer opportunities to get to know your customers. For example, if you are a bank teller, it's likely that you have access to their ID's where you can see their name. However, if this isn't the case, just introduce yourself and ask.

If you work in a Customer Service Call Center, a marketing department or any of the administrative areas of your company, it is also likely that you have access to more information about your customers. However, **the usefulness** of that information depends on your awareness of its importance and your decision to use it appropriately.

In any case, if you know more about the lives of the people you help, you will have a better chance of providing them with good service. If you know more about their **tastes and opinions**, you can better anticipate their needs and pleasantly surprise them. If you know more about their **preferences or the needs** they want to satisfy, then you can provide service that is artful and assertive.

Allow me to make a reference to an example I use in my courses:

If someone wants to buy a drill from you and you dismiss **the importance of knowing your customers better**, it's very likely that you will simply ask him or her, "What kind of drill would you like?" Otherwise, you would have to ask, "What kind of wall are you going to use it on and what size hole do you need to make?"

What that customer is really trying to fulfill is **an aspiration** other than the drill. Perhaps he or she needs to reattach a shelving unit, hang a lamp or mirror or redecorate a living room. The drill is merely a tool.

If you treat someone only as a buyer, it's harder to provide good service. However, **if you treat that customer like a human being**, you will ask all the necessary questions and make all the necessary comments to get to know him or her so you can better understand what he or she is really looking for.

46 | Cardinal sins of customer service

Although they may seem obvious, there are seven common poor service practices that lead to disappointed and disgruntled customers:

1. When you **don't keep** your promises.

2. When you disrespect and waste **their time**.

3. When you treat them with **indifference**, coldness, laziness or annoyance.

4. When you act **mechanically**, without bothering to listen attentively and really understand their needs.

5. When you **make excuses** for not helping them, blaming your coworkers or other departments.

6. When you help them as though you want to **get rid of them** quickly so they'll "leave you alone".

7. When you **dismiss them** as people or customers, either directly through labels and prejudices or indirectly through non-verbal cues and messages.

Any one of these sins by itself has a sufficiently negative impact to **upset** your customers to a high degree.

Even so, on more than a few occasions, customers fall victim to several of these sins simultaneously, perpetrated by various employees within the same company.

Think of these bad practices as if they were the main ingredients of a **poor service** banquet.

The more of these sins you commit, the angrier the customer will feel, and this, in turn, will make you feel just as angry if not even more so.

If you make a mistake, don't worry. The most important thing is that you focus on reacting artfully whenever you commit an error. In this regard, it would be a good idea for you to reread Practice #35.

47 | Replace the word "problem"

Acts of customer service are acts **of communication**. This is why it is so important that you pay attention to your language and the messages you transmit. They are the main tools of your trade.

There are words that put up barriers in interpersonal communication, unleash prejudices and complicate your work. They are expressions that have become **pet phrases**. Although they are said unconsciously or "innocently", they have a negative impact on communication.

One of these is the word "problem", which we use as a catchall for everything related to customer service, work in general or world relations.

In practical terms, the word "problem" has become **a label that hinders us** from realizing what customers' real needs are.

When a customer has a request, a question or a complaint, your mind works differently if you address those matters for what they are and not as "problems". If you treat them like "problems", it will always be more difficult for you to find **solutions** because you will be more focused on the negative connotations of the request or complaint.

Avoid negatively labeling the people and situations you deal with. **Call things what they really are**, so that you can confront them accordingly.

Instead of using the word "problem", try these other terms when applicable: situation, case, matter, need, request, question, challenge, opportunity, commitment, circumstance, opinion, demand, dissatisfaction, disappointment, proposal, inconvenience, requirement, condition, complaint, claim, submission, difficulty, etc.

Furthermore, **customers don't like** being treated like "problems". They consider it to be disrespectful and inconsiderate.

By replacing "problem" with words that have more precise and suitable meanings, you benefit from the intellectual effort that empowers **your intelligence** and enables you to regain control of your language and come up with more creative solutions.

48 | Express your will to help

Customers are very observant of the way you work because it **reveals** your concept of customer care.

They also observe your **vocabulary**. Don't think that this only has to do with simple expressions. British poet Samuel Johnson put it this way: "Language is the dress of thought" (http://bit.ly/awoFIQ).

The terms you use when you are helping people reveal what you think of them.

If you don't understand clearly that your work is to help people, as I mentioned in Practice #3, it will be hard for you to commit to your customers. Without commitment, your expressions become filled with **ambiguities** like: "Just a moment", "just a second", "hang on", "wait a minute" and "I'll help you in a little bit".

To customers, these messages are confusing and evasive. Keep in mind that the vagueness of these phrases can lead customers to **interpret or feel** that it annoys you to help them or that you have an unconcerned or indifferent attitude toward your work (or toward them).

Customers prefer more **precise** words that clearly demonstrate your true desire, interest, willingness, care and enthusiasm to help them.

Expressions like: "I'll take care of you immediately", "I'll be with you right away", or "I'm coming right now" are more **specific** and suitable for a customer service professional.

You demonstrate more willingness to serve when you answer a customer, "Of course!", "It would be my pleasure!" or "Right away", than when you use the ambiguous and common expression "Okay".

If you stop using the expression "Okay" and replace it with others that demonstrate much more **willingness** to help, you will exercise your language, your intelligence and your creativity, and at the same time you will communicate to your customers that you feel dignified by your work.

Always keep in mind that what you say and the way you say it has a significant impact on the way you think and act. Language isn't innocent.

49 | Stop saying "unfortunately"

The following are some of the generalized phrases for "politely" telling customers that you **aren't** going to help them:

—<u>Unfortunately</u>, we don't have that product.

—<u>Unfortunately</u>, there is nothing we can do for you.

—<u>Unfortunately</u>, our regulations and procedures don't permit us to do that.

—We would like to help you, but <u>unfortunately</u>, it's out of our hands.

Customers know that when they hear "unfortunately" it means that the person or company has "thrown in the towel" and doesn't understand that **the essence of customer care is helping** (an idea that is developed in the first 5 Practices in this book).

Helping customers is a type of commitment that requires **great courage**, even to the point of recommending a competitor that can provide them with something you can't at a given moment.

Feeling that a negative or sad situation is "unfortunate" has nothing to do with what it means to use the expression "unfortunately" as an excuse or justification for mediocrity or a lack of value.

If you tackle the **intellectual challenge** of avoiding saying "unfortunately", you give yourself a great opportunity to develop your intelligence and creativity, which will immediately improve your communication skills and the quality of service you give your customers.

The challenge ISN'T simply finding more "elegant" synonyms. If you deny service to a customer, there is no word that is sufficiently elegant or "refined" to make you look good.

To stop thinking and acting in terms of "unfortunately" and to make a positive difference to your customers, your best option is to **focus 100%** on what you can do and what is within your means in order to provide help and good service.

Please reread Practice #20 and #21.

50 | Be grateful

Thanking customers for their patronage isn't a customer service technique, but rather a gesture of **nobility, awareness and humility** on your part. However, it will only work if you are sincere and authentic (see Practice #14).

Being grateful to customers is also a way of reinforcing their importance and value to you. It keeps you alert and focused on people (two of the most difficult challenges in providing good customer care).

At the beginning and the end of your **interactions** with customers, you can say, "Thank you for stopping by", "Thank you for coming", "Thank you for being here", "Thank you for calling us", "Thank you for taking the time to write to us", "Thank you for letting me help you", or even "Thank you for your complaint and for giving us the opportunity to improve our service".

From this perspective of "conscious gratitude", your attitude and your communication with customers will reflect more professionalism and **willingness** to serve, behaviors that they will be especially thankful for.

A strong sense of gratitude toward customers reminds you that they are **the source** of your job and the foundation of any company or social organization.

Being grateful connects you with the necessary humility to focus on serving people with dignity.

By "humility" I don't mean timidity or submissiveness, but instead respect and dedication to people.

Remember that when you feel **dignity** in the act of serving and helping someone, you reaffirm your humanity.

When you are authentically grateful, this also motivates customers to believe and trust you more.

Expressions like "Thank you for stopping by. Please come back soon" leave the doors open to **your future** and help you cultivate long-term relationships with your customers.

Final thoughts

Many companies, social organizations and State institutions don't know what they can do to make the customer care training they give their personnel *more effective*. They feel that a good part of their investment in this area fails to achieve the desired objectives.

The courses and workshops on the subject usually have **fleeting results**. Most of the participants in those training sessions return to their jobs with a lot of enthusiasm, but in general this excitement doesn't last very long.

The reasons for this are varied and are related to the individuals in each organization. However, there are three reasons that are common to all of the cases I have worked on over the past 20 years:

First reason: Customer care training tends to be very limited and inconsistent.

It's a topic that is underestimated to such an extent that not even educational institutions include it in their curriculum, in spite of the fact that in society it is considered to be a cultural matter of vital importance.

The traditional approach in organizational training doesn't anticipate the need for continuous training in customer care. This is why in this book I have insisted on art as a model: training never ceases and neither does practice.

Second reason: The approach used in training emphasizes customer service as a question of techniques and attitudes.

There's no doubt that these are very important aspects, but they aren't the basis of good customer care. Attitudes and techniques are a consequence of people's values related to their work and their future vision of it.

Third reason: Organizations don't tend to be very consistent or constant in applying the same principles to their personnel (their internal customers) that they demand them to apply to their external customers.

This lack of consistency ends up translating into an approach to customer care through superficial initiatives without continuity. The result is that organizations fail to cultivate a higher level of professionalism in that area over time.

What do I suggest for making customer care training more sustainable over time?

I recommend the following strategic guidelines:

First: Customer care must be taken up as a question of the organization's **culture**. This means that it should be a fundamental component of the organization's mission and vision.

An organization's culture consists of the most common daily behaviors on the part of its members. As such, this culture is formed whether or not there is a plan for it and whether or not the organization's leaders are aware of it.

So, organizations always have the opportunity to promote a culture geared toward dignifying and rewarding good customer service. However, this vision requires a concrete action plan in order to sow the seeds of the **desired** culture, harvest it and sustain it over time.

Second: The **principle leaders** of an organization are primarily responsible for its culture. They play the leading roles in the organizational culture and all related training and maintenance.

CEO's, Vice-Presidents and Managers must head up all initiatives for customer care training.

That's the only way they will truly understand the strategic necessity for a model of service **leadership** in their business that effectively outlines the values of good service from day to day.

Third: Customer care training must be a **part of daily operations**. In this way the organization guarantees the formation of good habits (culture) and the preservation and consolidation of those habits over time.

Isolated, sporadic training sessions don't develop the "muscles of customer care". It's the same thing that happens if you only go to the gym or exercise once-in-a-while: you can't stay in consistently good shape.

"Exercising" the values that characterize good customer care is a more strategic and effective method than the traditional approach of a "light bulb" of motivation and knowledge that usually takes the form of isolated lectures, courses and workshops.

In this respect, in the first part of this book, there's a chapter entitled "Why 50 practices?" My goal is for these to serve as a guide for incorporating a simple method of artistic training into your daily activities.

This is only a general outline of the three strategic guidelines that I consider to be indispensable for getting the most out of an investment in customer care training.

The practical details of these guidelines depend on how each organization adapts and expands on these ideas, in accordance with its specific characteristics and circumstances.

I will conclude this book by expressing my sincere wish that it be truly useful as a reference for your daily to-do list.

Thank you very much for taking the time to read it. I would also appreciate it if you write to me with any comments on the experience you have had with this book.

Juan Carlos Jiménez
jucar@cograf.com
December, 2010

As an epilogue

Considering his extensive professional experience in various service companies, I asked my valued friend, Alexis Perez, for a commentary on this book, and he provided me with this interesting and very fitting reflection, which I would like to share with all of you:

"I don't believe in good service"

I don't believe in good service, just like I don't believe in "good saints" or "good miracles". A saint, like a miracle, can only be good. In the same way, service can only be good. If it isn't good, then it isn't service. It might be some other type of relationship or contact between a customer and the person waiting on him or her, but it cannot and must not be qualified as "service".

Ranking levels of service turns it into something relative and reduces it to imprecise categories.

Throughout my experience in the corporate world, I have spent hours in large national and international companies, observing up close how their personnel perform, both when faced with customers' needs and in relation to their specific job duties.

They limit themselves almost exclusively to "waiting on" customers, but not serving them. This has had a significant negative impact on the customer experience. It has almost completely destroyed that sacred temple constructed on the foundation of close, trusting relationships with those who are the sustenance of every commercial and company endeavor.

Customers don't want to be sold something. They don't want to buy something. The only thing they want is to satisfy a need and reap the benefits stemming from that decision. Providing a service means fulfilling that wish in a pleasant and advantageous way.

However, this isn't always accomplished. Few companies have arrived at a full understanding of the true significance of service, and this is evident even in their manuals, in which, ironically, they speak of "good service".

They have also failed to completely understand the enormous responsibility that rests on the shoulders of their personnel, especially their sales teams.

They invest very little in training them, they pay them poorly, they have the worst possible systems, if any at all, for tracking their performance and, most importantly, they lack adequate reward systems for stimulating excellence in those who have a direct relationship with customers.

This book, the fruit of Juan Carlos Jimenez's invaluable experience, explores this topic in depth. With humility, simplicity and complete mastery, he introduces us to concepts, ideas and discoveries of enormous importance.

In 50 practices, he summarizes the basics, fortifying them with the findings he has compiled during his extensive experience in the challenging world of customer service.

Juan Carlos goes over the obvious, the essentials, the simple steps and the daily ins and outs of the experience we have with our customers.

He doesn't attempt to turn service into a complicated equation, but instead does just the opposite, reducing it to its purest expression: 1) Service is provided by people; 2) Service is provided to people; and, in conclusion 3) It is something that happens between people. That's what it's all about.

I believe that this book makes an invaluable contribution toward perfecting the work of those who provide customer service and it does so in a way that is so instructive and agreeable that I am sure that the reader will grasp the material immediately and put it into practice.

Perhaps he or she will discover that it isn't magic or training that makes the difference in customer service, but rather the commitment that we all must have to the work we do and the people we serve.

Alexis Pérez

Recommended Reading

ALBRECHT, Karl (1995). *At America's Service: How Your Company Can Join the Customer Service Revolution.* USA: Grand Central Publishing.

BALLARD, Jim; FINCH, Fred (2004). *Customer Mania: It's never too late to build a customer-focused company* USA: Free Press.

BECKWITH, Harry (2010). *What Clients Love.* USA: Business Plus.

BLANCHARD, Ken (2007). *Know Can Do!* USA: Berrett-Koehler Publishers.

BLANCHARD, Ken; BOWLES, Sheldon (1998). *Raving fans.* USA: Harper Collins.

BRINKMAN, Rick; KIRSHNER, Rick (2005). *Love Thy Customer.* USA: McGraw-Hill.

CAPODAGLI, Bill (2006). *The Disney Way. Harnessing the management secrets of Disney in your company.* USA: McGraw-Hill.

CARNEGIE, Dale (2009). *How to Win Friends and Influence People.* USA: Simon & Schuster.

CIALDINI, Robert; GOLDSTEIN, Noah; MARTIN, Steve (2008). *Yes!: 50 Scientifically Proven Ways to Be Persuasive.* USA: Free Press.

CRAVEN, Robert (2005). *Customer Is King.* USA: Virgin Books.

CROTHER, Cyndi (2004). *Catch. Afishmonger's Guide to Greatness.* San Francisco: Berret-Koehler Publishers.

ELIAS, Joan (2000). *Clientes contentos de verdad. Claves para comprender a clientes y a usuarios.* [Truly Happy Customers. Keys to Understanding Customers and Users] Barcelona: Ediciones Gestión 2000.

HEWARD, Lyn (2006). *The Spark: Igniting the Creative Fire that Lives within Us All.* USA: Doubleday.

JIMENEZ, Juan Carlos (2008). *The Significance of Values in an Organization.* Caracas: Cograf Ediciones.

JIMENEZ, Juan Carlos (2011). *Increase Your Opportunities. Paradigms for Personal Motivation.* Caracas: Cograf Ediciones.

KINNI, Ted (2003). *Be our guest: Perfecting the art of customer service.* USA: Disney Editions.

LUNDIN, Stephen; PAUL, Harry; CHRISTENSEN, John (2000). *Fish!* USA: Hyperion.

MITCHEL, Jack (2003). *Hug Your Customers.* USA: Hyperion.

SEIDMAN, Dov (2007). *How: why how we do anything means everything... in business (and in life).* New Jersey: John Wiley & Sons.

About the author

Juan Carlos Jimenez is advertiser and
entrepreneur. Consultant in marketing and
corporate communications.

Began his professional career in 1978 as a graphic
designer. He has worked as a Creative Director in
publishing companies, printed communications
media, design studios and advertising agencies.

In 1990, he founded Cograf Comunicaciones,
where he works in the areas of brand identity project design and
execution, corporate image, sales and marketing, customer service,
Internet business and strategic planning.

He also develops training programs aimed at promoting a culture of
customer care and the formation of high-performance work teams,
based on values of personal and professional excellence.

He is the author of several the management books: E-mail at the
workplace, The significance of values in an organization, Increase
your opportunities, and Dialogue 2 point 0, among others. See all on
Amazon.com: http://amzn.to/nJFEGm

He has been an invited professor at various universities in Venezuela,
giving lectures on marketing and strategic communications.

He continuously shares his ideas and recommendations in numerous
seminars, conferences and corporate events throughout Venezuela
and other countries where he has been an invited speaker.

Email: jucar@cograf.com
Facebook.com/jucarjim
Twitter: @jucarjim

Books published by Cograf Inc.

Get them on Amazon.com: http://amzn.to/nJFEGm

Cograf Inc.:
Publishing and Consulting

We are a company formed by specialists in corporate communications, "internal marketing" and training.

Since 1990 we had helpeld bussines of different sizes, increasing their team productivity, based on develped excellence in customer care values, in a very innovative training sesions.

Our roots are Hispanic, and we have a comprehensive vision about our idiosyncrasie. So, we know how to encourage latin american people to assume the personal challenges of good customer care and passion for excellence that competitive market requiere today.

We design training programs, tailored to meet needs and conditions of each company, using thought-provoking content and a significative learning methodology procces.

Also, we can publish our managment books with the logo of your company on the cover, and a preface text of your company.

Our publishing services include:
* Interior book layout (black and white or full-color).
* Cover design.
* ISBN number.
* Industry-satandadr trim sizes.
* Professional binding.
* Low author copies prices.
* e-Books.
* Editorial and marketing consulting.

Contact us for more information: 5379 Lyons Rd, PMB 198. Coconut Creek, FL 33073. Phone (954) 530-4452.

www.cograf.com

www.cursoscograf.com

www.libroscograf.com

www.internetips.com

www.folletoweb.com

cograf.wordpress.com

facebook.com/cograf

twitter.com/cograf

www.artesupremo.com

www.ampliatusoportunidades.com

www.elvalordelosvalores.com

www.dialogo2punto0.com